CRITICAL THINKING SKILLS

Marcia Heiman

Joshua Slomianko

nea PROFESSIONAL LIBRARY
National Education Association
Washington, D.C.

To *Jeanne S. Chall*, in grateful appreciation for her support and encouragement over many long years.

—M. H.

J. S.

Copyright 1986,1985
National Education Association of the United States

Printing History

First Printing:	May 1985
Second Printing:	February 1986
Third Printing:	March 1989
Fourth Printing:	September 1991

Note

The opinions expressed in this publication should not be construed as representing the policy or position of the National Education Association. Materials published as part of the Analysis and Action Series are intended to be discussion documents for teachers who are concerned with specialized interests of the profession.

Library of Congress Cataloging in Publication Data

Heiman, Marcia.
  Critical thinking skills.

  (Analysis and action series)
  Bibliography: p.
  1. Cognition in children. 2. Decision-making in children. 3. Problem solving in children.
  I. Slomianko, Joshua. II. Title. III. Series.
LB 1062.5.H44 1985   370.15'2   85–5118
ISBN 0-8106-1693-9

CONTENTS

The Authors

Marcia Heiman is Director, Learning to Learn Program, Boston College, Chestnut Hill, Massachusetts.

Joshua Slomianko is Co-Director, Learning Skills Consultants, Cambridge, Massachusetts.

FOREWORD

Can our schools truly help every student "master" what is taught? I believe they can. Scholars today understand—far better than before—what it takes to learn.

Harvard Education Dean Patricia Graham points out that current research on learning theory is substantial and impressive. She insists that "the moment is now right for the transition from scholarship to practice, from studying to action." I agree.

Our intent is to move students from passive spectatorship to active classroom involvement.

Mastery demands that students go far beyond rote memorization. It requires a higher order of thinking, particularly the ability to analyze, to synthesize, to formulate probing questions. A student who has achieved academic mastery can graft theory to practice—integrate subject matter with real-world experiences. Mastery empowers a student to deal constructively with the world outside the classroom door.

—Mary Hatwood Futrell
President, NEA
February 1986

SIX PROFESSIONAL DEVELOPMENT WORKSHOPS FOR IMPROVING STUDENTS' THINKING SKILLS

Developed by Marcia Heiman and Joshua Slomianko, for NEA

1. What is critical thinking?

   Objective: Teachers will brainstorm definitions of critical thinking skills, using the NEA materials as guideposts. Other questions addressed in this workshop will be: what can critical thinking skills do for the learner? what do people need to begin to use critical thinking skills?

2. Using questioning techniques

   Objective: Teachers will identify the kinds of teacher- and student-generated questions that facilitate different levels of thinking, from factual recall to analysis and evaluation.

3. Creativity in the classroom

   Objective: Teachers will explore methods for encouraging divergent thinking in students, so that students learn to go beyond the facts and imagine possibilities and connections that may not currently exist.

4. Active learning

   Objective: Teachers will identify practices for encouraging increased student participation and student-centered learning while practicing thinking-skills exercises.

5. Classroom management

   Objective: Teachers will discuss methods of rewarding student creativity, giving students feedback on progress, and maintaining a high level of student productivity as a critical component of thinking skills development.

6. Applying critical thinking skills to the content-area classroom

   Objective: Teachers will learn how to encourage and develop critical thinking skills in a variety of academic disciplines, including English/language arts, social studies, mathematics, and science.

(Contact NEA for complete information about the professional development program.)

WHAT IS CRITICAL THINKING?

Whenever you ask yourself, "What is critical thinking?" reflect on what you, as a good learner, do when you are listening or reading for information. In the course of this reflection, you will find the skill that is basic to critical thinking: engaging in an internal dialogue. For example, if you attend a lecture titled "Should Teachers Support Prayer in the School?" you bring with you many questions from your own experience. You listen to the speaker *actively*: that is, you anticipate his/her comments and continually "test" them during the lecture—"Do I agree with this position? Is that statement true, given what I have seen in the classroom? How do I personally feel about what is being said?"

You will find it more difficult to listen actively, however, if you attend a theoretical lecture to which you bring only practical background knowledge. For example, imagine planning to attend a lecture titled "Effects of Semantic Integration Training on the Recall of Pictograph Sentences by Children in Kindergarten and First Grade" (33).* In a situation like this you will find that you work a little harder at the internal dialogue process. Before deciding to attend, you say to yourself, "If I'm going to understand this lecture, I'll have to translate it into words I'm familiar with. Let's see. 'Semantic integration'. In English grammar, 'semantics' has something to do with meaning. 'Integration' might mean seeing how the parts of something are related. 'Pictograph sentences' are probably stories told in pictures, like those picture books used in Ethel Green's kindergarten class. That's it: they're trying to see what effects teaching young children to read picture stories has on their understanding and recall of the stories."

---

*Numbers in parentheses appearing in the text refer to the Bibliography beginning on page 44.

By engaging in this internal dialogue, you are demonstrating important skills: raising questions, breaking up a complex idea into components, drawing on your own prior knowledge, translating complicated ideas into examples. The hypothesis you generate about the lecture title—that it will present research information about some important prereading skills—may motivate you to attend. That is, you may wish to attend in order to get feedback on whether the lecture does in fact deal with the topic you envision. In anticipation, you recall other evidence—from your teaching experience or a university class—bearing on the topic. You therefore arrive at the lecture with a series of hypotheses about its content.

In other words, you are engaged in the process of *critical thinking*.

Your problem as a teacher is to encourage your students—who may not have relevant background knowledge to call on, and who may not have much experience in carrying on such a dialogue about school-related subjects—to progress through stages similar to those you went through when deciding to attend the lecture on children's comprehension of picture books.

This monograph reviews research on the development of critical thinking skills and introduces a series of these skills that can be incorporated into your classroom teaching. The activities presented can be used by teachers across grade levels and disciplines.

"We must help students develop analytical thinking skills—and the ability to make judgments.

Tomorrow's world will be truly international, and the culture schools transmit won't be solely ours. We can't live on an island called America."

Mary Hatwood Futrell
President, NEA
November 16, 1985

EFFORTS TO IMPROVE STUDENTS' THINKING SKILLS

For more than a decade, a number of educators and psychologists have looked at learning from a new perspective: rather than testing and labeling students by ability and achievement, they have sought ways to *improve* students' basic reasoning skills. This represents a significant shift away from the nature/nurture controversy: the assumption of these researchers and clinicians has been that critical thinking represents a set of skills that can improve with practice. The questions posed by this work are as follows: what are the most important thinking skills, and how can they be most effectively enhanced?

This section reviews both research findings and several programs for improving students' thinking skills.

HELPING STUDENTS REMEMBER WHAT THEY READ

The first well-controlled studies investigating factors affecting verbal learning were done in the area of reading research in the late 1960's through the mid-1970's. Several studies showed that questions generated by text authors improve students' recall of text material (32, 31, 13, 2). Further, other researchers found that *student*-generated questions were effective in improving student reading recall and comprehension (18, 34). Moreover, Andre and Anderson found that training students to generate questions had the secondary effect of improving the *quality* of the questions (1). They also found that the effects of question generating were stronger for students with poor entry skills than for those with initially good skills. Discussing this latter finding, they hypothesized that "high verbal ability students already have the component skills included in the self-questioning study technique" (1). That is, it may be that successful learners read to answer questions as a matter of course. By teaching unsuccessful students to raise questions as they read, these researchers helped them to acquire what may be a critical skill for learning complex verbal material.

HELPING STUDENTS IMPROVE PROBLEM-SOLVING SKILLS

Externalizing the Thinking Process

This clue, that the key to improving thinking lies in the examination of successful students' learning strategies, has become central to the work of a number of researchers who have investigated students' problem-solving methods, often outside the laboratory. Several of these researchers have concentrated on developing models of prototypical good and poor problem-solving behavior. Gray (19) speaks of "identifying good habits of thought" by studying "ideal" thought patterns. Wales's Guided Design (39) teaches students to solve open-ended problems aloud in small groups, using ordered steps and receiving feedback from the professor. An integral part of the work of these researchers is obtaining problem-solving protocols of novices and experts via taped interviews. Using this method, Larkin (27) found that beginning physics students initially rely on formulas, while experts construct pictorial models of problems. Lin (28) talks about the difficulties in constructing good models of problem-solving in novices and experts. Greeno (20), working with high school geometry students, has refined the model-building process through computer simulation: the data fed into his computer was taken from thinking-aloud protocols given by students studying geometry. More recently, he has analyzed the counting tasks of young children, building a theory of children's "conceptual competence" from his data (21). Clement (9), also using taped interviews with students, has constructed a model of knowledge, assumptions, and preconceptions that beginning students and experts bring to the solution of problems in physics.

An important intervention to emerge from this group of psychologists has been developed by Whimbey and Lochhead (43). Building in an early experiment by Bloom and Broder (4), they have devised a set of procedures that teach initially poor problem solvers to be increasingly more systematic in their thinking. From their observations of students' thinking-aloud protocols, Whimbey and Lochhead have drawn the following conclusions:

- The critical learning strategies of good learners can be identified by asking them to think aloud when solving problems.
- Initially poor problem solvers can acquire improved problem-solving skills by systematically analyzing problems aloud, often working in pairs.

10

- It appears that an important skill in good problem solving is generating and testing hypotheses—a finding that reinforces other work on the role of questions in learning.

- When initially poor problem solvers master the skills of systematic problem analysis through exercises, this skill is transferable to other learning situations; they have learned to think better.

The training method developed by Whimbey and Lochhead, Cognitive Process Instruction, helps unsuccessful learners become more systematic in their problem solving. Working in pairs, as active listeners and problem solvers (see pp. 37–38), students proceed through a series of word problems that become increasingly more complex, similar to complex word problems on intelligence tests. The following problem exemplifies those used in their system:

Cross out the letter after the letter in the word "pardon" that is in the same position in the word as it is in the alphabet.

Successful problem solvers would work through the problem, asking themselves a set of questions:

Okay, so I have to cross out a letter which is in the same position in the word as it is in the alphabet. "P" is in the first position in the word "pardon." But "a" is in the first position in the alphabet. In the word "pardon," "a" is in the second position, "r" is in the third position. Okay, "d" is in the fourth position in the word and it's also in the fourth position in the alphabet. But now in the beginning of the problem, there was something confusing. Let me go back to it. I have to cross out the letter *after* the letter in the word "pardon." So I have to cross out the ʳer after the "d"—cross out the letter "o." (41, p. 19)

In contrast, poor problem solvers, who do badly on SAT exams and IQ tests, will skip over much of the relevant information, guess at answers, and fail to check systematically to assess their answers.

The Whimbey/Lochhead exercises force students to externalize their thinking—to think aloud, where errors and skipped steps can be readily identified; in addition, working in pairs helps students learn to edit unsystematic thinking in themselves and others. The exercises are particularly effective when they are given in preparation for complex problem-solving courses, such as mathematics, chemistry, or physics. Students learn to transfer the skills acquired in the exercises to their problem solving in these courses.

There is evidence that this approach is effective. Hunter and others

(25), working at a predominantly Black college, report that the Whimbey/Lochhead system results in significantly improved SAT scores and ability to complete science programs in college.

Nonverbal Problem Solving

As we have indicated, the Whimbey/Lochhead exercises are similar to items on verbal intelligence tests. In contrast, a number of programs aimed at improving students' thinking focus on exercises similar to nonverbal intelligence test items. They require the manipulation of abstract symbols and forms. For example, an instructional item might contain a series of geometric forms; the student is asked to complete the series by choosing a form that is similar, or analogous, to the figures in the original line (see Figure 1).

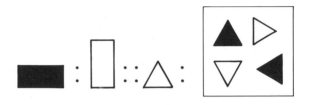

Which figure completes the analogy?
Figure 1

The authors of these programs maintain that the skills they intend to teach—classification, finding analogies, tracing sequences, etc.—can be taught only in content-free instructional settings. They contend that if students learn the skills in isolation, they will be most likely to use them in a variety of situations.

The most widely used program of this kind is Feuerstein's Instrumental Enrichment. The exercises in this program, which students work on individually or in a small group with an adult "mediator," are aimed at improving learners' general intellectual abilities: "Instrumental Enrichment (IE) represents an attempt at intervention designed to aid the retarded performer to accede to higher levels of cognitive functioning by changing his cognitive structure rather than affecting his manifest behavior" (16, p. 1). In other words, the student working through the IE exercises will develop general thinking skills that will translate into improved intellectual performance.

The Organization of Dots exercises exemplify IE training. In these exercises, students are asked to find geometric shapes in an apparently random field of dots. Once the shape is identified, the student is asked to connect the relevant dots, thereby highlighting the hidden square, triangle, or rectangle. (The exercises are similar to "connect-the-dots" games found in children's magazines, except that they use progressively more complex arrangements of geometric forms.) Feuerstein maintains that these exercises give students "practice in the projection of virtual relationships . . . [providing] opportunities for the performance of a number of cognitive operations: differentiation, segregation, organization by restructuring the field" (15).

We have several reservations about these kinds of programs. The chief problem relates to transfer of training: it is unclear what effects nonverbal, abstract exercises have on academic learning. These programs make the assumption that, since nonverbal intelligence test items are highly correlated with general intellectual ability, the way to improve general intellectual functioning is to train students to perform well on such items. It may be that the reverse is true: that is, people who have good verbal intellectual skills, who tend to perform well academically, perform well on nonverbal tests as a by-product of their good verbal thinking skills. They "talk" to themselves when solving problems such as the figural analogy on p. 12 of this monograph (for example, "Let's see. There are two rectangles in the first group, one white and one black . . . ").*

The advocates of nonverbal conceptual training programs believe that students can acquire new thinking skills only in content-free learning situations. Therefore, teachers of their systems are not immediately encouraged to apply related strategies (for example, finding the main idea in a paragraph, which is said to be analogous to finding a figure in a maze of dots) to academic learning. In programs such as IE, students work through nonverbal problems for months. Only after demonstrating mastery on exercises such as the Organization of Dots are connections made to content-related material.

It may be that any academic gains students make in these programs are directly attributable to the "transfer" activities constructed by inventive teachers—such as having students look for similar and differ-

---

*It may be that, if students worked on such problems in pairs, talking aloud their thinking, the exercises might improve students' abilities to work through problems more systematically than they have in the past. The Whimbey/Lochhead program, which uses pair problem solving and whose problems are language-based, requires less transfer to actual academic problem solving.

ent elements in reading material or identify key concepts. In other words, it may be that such academic gains would occur without the weeks and months of prior, abstract, "conceptual" training.

Divergent Thinking

Some efforts at improving students' thinking call for "divergent thinking" in a recitation format. In these exercises, students are called on to stretch their imaginations, to look at familiar situations in a new way. The most widely used program of this kind was created by deBono, who constructed a set of content-free exercises or "operations" designed to improve students' thinking (11). deBono is concerned with what he calls the "perceptual," as distinct from the "processing," phase of thinking—that is, areas where logical analysis is less helpful, where discovery of new approaches is of paramount importance. He correctly points out that the teaching of logic is a limited approach to improving thinking, since logic is confined to the analysis of totally specified problems. The exercises deBono suggests are simple and clear. In the PMI exercise (Plus, Minus, Interest), for example, students are asked to evaluate a proposition according to its positive and negative aspects, as well as those that seem interesting. Working alone or in small groups, students might be asked to consider positive, negative, and interesting sides of the proposition "All cars should be painted yellow." In another deBono exercise, CAF (Consider All Factors), students are asked to generate increasingly longer lists of aspects of a given situation or proposition.

We believe that the chief value of these kinds of exercises is to enable students to "loosen up," to allow themselves to think of unusual ways of looking at information and expressing ideas. This kind of exercise could well be a first step in more complex decision-making exercises (see pp. 39–41).

deBono, however, claims a wider effect for his exercises. He maintains that they provide students with tools that can be transferred to any problem-solving situation. He believes that these skills must be learned independent of any content-area information, that only in such isolation can the process of thinking be developed:

"If a person is thinking about something then surely he is learning how to think."

Unfortunately, this is not true. A geography teacher would claim that in learning geography a pupil would be forced to think. A history teacher and a science teacher would make the same claim. All would be right. The question is whether thinking about something develops any transferable skill in thinking. In content subjects . . . there is comparatively little scope for thinking except for the hindsight variety: "Now you can see that this happened because of that . . . " This is no fault of the teacher. It is the nature of content subjects that is at fault. (11)

In short, deBono, like Feuerstein, subscribes to the notion that intellectual skills must be sharpened in *isolation* from content-area issues—that thinking skills will be most widely applied by the student if they are initially practiced in content-free settings.

We believe there is a critical weakness in this line of argument: it implies that no one has ever thought creatively in a content area, that academic learning itself is somehow suspect. This criticism is too far-reaching. It may be that the way students are taught at present is too fact-oriented, that the play of ideas in any discipline is not stressed in most of formal education. However, the fields themselves raise questions that stretch the creative powers of scientists and researchers. Perhaps instead of abandoning academic disciplines as sources for creative thinking in schools, we need to learn to teach them in ways that involve students in the questions raised by the fields, so they can sense the excitement of the scientist at work.

Incorporating Thinking Skills Instruction into the Content Classroom

The idea that students can adapt more complex learning tools than rote memory to academic learning—that they can "learn how to learn"—has gained increasing currency in educational circles. Newspaper articles report stories of teachers who have successfully promoted active learning in their students; a number of states are mandating the teaching of thinking skills in public schools. The Learning to Learn system, perhaps the most comprehensive thinking-improvement system now available, exemplifies successful efforts of this kind (22, 23). Developed originally for disadvantaged college students, LTL has been used effectively for students reading as low as at fifth-grade level. The system is based on the work of a group of researchers and clinicians at the University of Michigan during the 1960's. Working under Dale M. Brethower, the group—like the psychologists mentioned earlier—sought to discover what was systematic and predictable about successful students' learning. These thinking strategies were identified by asking students to make internal events external and explicit—to think aloud as they engaged in a variety of academic tasks.

The group found that successful students commonly use the following major learning tools. They—

- ask questions of new materials, engaging in a covert dialogue with the author or listener, forming hypotheses, reading or listening for confirmation;
- identify the component parts of complex principles and ideas, breaking down major tasks into smaller units;
- devise informal feedback mechanisms to assess their own progress in learning; and
- focus on instructional objectives, identifying and directing their study behaviors to meet course objectives.

The originators of LTL "translated" these skills into exercises that less successful students could apply directly to their academic work. Results included significantly improved grades and retention in school; improved reading, writing, and listening skills; and increased student motivation. Classrooms incorporating LTL methods are active learning environments with a great deal of student participation.

The Learning to Learn system contains general learning skills, which can be applied to the study of any content area, and subject-specific skills, which are dictated by the structure of specific academic disciplines. The following provides an overview of the system:

Input
Stage: Generating questions from lecture notes; reading to answer questions (textbooks and books without headings); reading to solve problems; reading for examples; reading graphs, tables, and diagrams; developing editing checklists to improve grammar in writing and to work through math-based problems.

Organiza-
tion Stage: Information mapping, flow charting, using task checklists.

Output
Stage: Writing to answer questions, systematic problem-solving, developing keyword diagrams.

The system provides both "left brain," analytical exercises, and "right brain," creative exercises. Students do not view the skills as separate ones; rather, they come to see all the LTL exercises as variations of two central skills: generating questions and breaking down ideas and tasks into manageable parts. As they become more familiar with the skills, students "play" with the ideas presented in their classes and reading assignments: they make variations on assigned problems, they ask themselves questions that were raised—but not necessarily answered—by the material, they construct maps that show the relationships between apparently unrelated ideas and facts in their courses. Unlike study skills, which lose their effect after the student stops explicitly using them, the LTL skills become part of the learner, integral to the individual's thinking process. The system's developers see LTL as comprising a fourth basic skill, reasoning, which facilitates the acquisition of the other three—reading, writing, and arithmetic (23).

LEARNING STYLES

No review of critical thinking is complete without a discussion of the "learning styles" issue. There is a good deal of evidence that students learn in somewhat different ways—some are more analytical, others more wholistic in their approach to new information; some learn better when working independently, others require direction. There is evidence that differences in learning style may affect skill in reading (8), language acquisition (5), learning mathematical concepts (12), and even moral development (24).

What lessons does this research have for teachers who wish to promote critical thinking skills in their students? Many researchers exploring the problem of learning styles advise educators to teach toward students' strengths. Cleland (8), for example, suggests that reading clinics diagnose for students' strengths and build strengths-instruction into lesson planning. This is very sound advice: students will more likely practice a skill on their own if it gives them feelings of competence and mastery.

"Teaching to strengths" can have a negative effect, however, if students' weaknesses are ignored. An extreme case recently appeared in a school where one of the authors acted as a critical thinking-skills consultant. When a teacher began an exercise in generating questions from lecture notes, one student objected that he could take notes only from the blackboard. The student's Individual Educational Plan had specified that he was a visual learner, and he had been "protected" from learning experiences requiring good auditory processing skills. A better educational plan would have required exercises that enabled the student to build the skills he was lacking.

In practice, no teacher can be all things to all students. Perhaps the best way for teachers to incorporate "learning styles" research findings into the classroom is to be aware that students have many different, individual approaches to learning. Vary activities to allow for such individual expression and skills: make both structured and open-ended assignments, ask students to work independently and in pairs, ask students to find specific supporting arguments in a debate on a controversial issue, and ask students to imagine future worlds resulting from discoveries not yet made. By varying critical thinking assignments, teachers will tap the skills and remediate the skill deficits of most students.

"Finding the right answer is important, of course. But more important is developing the ability to see that problems have multiple solutions, that getting from X to Y demands basic skills and mental agility, imagination, persistence, patience."

Mary Hatwood Futrell
President, NEA
May 5, 1985

IMPROVING STUDENTS' CRITICAL THINKING SKILLS: SOME EXERCISES

This section presents a number of exercises that you can use to stimulate your students' critical thinking in the classroom. We urge you to experiment: try our methods, modify them as you see fit, test out those that seem to work for your students, share your ideas with your colleagues. While doing this, keep in mind the following general guidelines:

- Make your critical thinking skills exercises *relevant* to your students. If they are working toward solving problems that interest them, they will be more involved in the learning process.

- In both critical thinking exercises and the structure of your classroom, find ways to make learning an *active* process for your students.

- Help students use problem-solving methods that prevent them from *skipping steps*—ask them to work in pairs, talking aloud their thinking, or to draw models of the problem.

- When introducing a new set of concepts, always show students both the *big picture* (so that they can see the relationship between disparate facts) and ways to break down a complex idea into its *component parts*.

- Focus on the problem-solving *process*, not the memorization of facts.

- Find ways to individually *reinforce* your students for their approximations to appropriate performance.

The exercises presented here were originally designed for use with students in the middle grades through high school. However, teachers of early elementary students may find that these techniques can be modified for their students. For example, question-generating exercises can be used at all levels of instruction. As Bruner has said, "The task of teaching a subject to a child at any particular age is one of representing the structure of that subject in terms of the child's way of viewing things." (6, p. 33). For example, teachers can introduce the concepts of supply and demand to kindergarten students by organizing a classroom "store," and by using question-generating exercises related to students' activities in the store.

Some of the exercises in this section are progressive: they begin with "translation" question exercises and proceed to complex decision-making exercises. Others are designed to be used in conjunction with all exercises: providing students' with information feedback as a method of ongoing positive reinforcement, providing students with models and foils of completed critical thinking exercises, and grouping students in ways that will facilitate active learning. Finally, we encourage you to make your own variations on our suggestions.

GENERATING QUESTIONS

The process of generating questions is fundamental to critical thinking: it is the basis of the ongoing internal dialogue that is the core of intellectual analysis. Most teachers know this, and attempt to encourage it in their students, but they are frequently disappointed with the results. We feel that question generating is most useful when it promotes *active student learning*. However, for a variety of reasons, many teachers have been trained to use instructional methods that produce a passive learning environment. This section discusses various aspects of student question generating. To give you a clear sense of what we mean by active learning, we contrast each active approach with its opposite—one that may increase student passivity.

1. *Stimulating question generating*

Active Learning: Experiment with ways of helping your students "translate" material from books, discussions, lectures, and films into questions.

Example: Mr. Howard has just shown his fifth grade class a film on the steel industry. The film illustrated the mining and refining of ore and the forging of steel, which was then made into parts of familiar products, like automobiles. After the film, Mr. Howard asks students to work in pairs and make lists of the stages of steel production they have just seen. When students have written as much as they can remember, he asks them to look at what they have written as a series of answers on a test, and (still working in pairs) to write the imaginary test questions for these "answers."

Working with the class as a whole, Mr. Howard then asks students to read the questions to him. The questions, which he puts on the board, become the basis for a discussion of the film.

Discussion: Questions provide a frame of reference for students to organize the facts they learn. While it is difficult to retain isolated facts, information organized into a pattern is more easily recalled and applied. When students learn the kinds of questions a field asks, they have a framework in which to put the new information.

Starting with "translation" questions helps students build this skill. Since they are new to most fields they are studying, they cannot begin by asking creative, explanatory questions. However, once students have begun to generate questions, a natural process occurs in which they begin to see the field they are studying in terms of the kinds of questions it raises—and they start the process of asking their own questions about the material.

Passive Learning: Don't expect students to be able to begin generating questions by coming up with questions reflecting their interest in the subject matter.

Example: Mr. Rudd asked his tenth grade class to read a chapter on Greek city states. He begins the class by asking students if they have any questions about the chapter. There is no response. Feeling slightly exasperated, as he usually does, given evidence of students' ignoring reading assignments, Mr. Rudd sighs and gives a brief lecture on the key points of the chapter. He describes the geography of the Greek islands and the development of separate city states. His lecture over, Mr. Rudd asks if students have any questions about it. Silence. Mr. Rudd then begins calling on students, asking them questions about the material he has just covered.

Discussion: Many teachers feel that the easiest questions for students to raise are those that reflect students' concerns. It is true that students will be more highly motivated to learn content that interests them— that answers questions they bring to class. However, it does *not* follow that early question-raising attempts should focus on students' inventiveness/skills as question askers. Students have been conditioned over long years not to expect course material to mirror their interests. When

21

Ruthie is asked by Mr. Relty what questions she has about school-related material, she will likely come up with a blank. Her internal response to the question "Students, do you have any questions about what we've been studying?" is, "What does Mr. Relty want me to say?"

It is difficult to engage the student's imagination in generating questions (those of interest to the *student*) in part because students are not used to their questions forming the basis of academic learning. However, perhaps more significantly, students often cannot "come up with" questions because what they are studying is, by definition, new to them. In the initial phases of study, they have difficulty asking questions because they are novices: *they do not know which questions the field answers.*

2. Improving reading skills through question generating

Issues of reading comprehension are important when discussing critical thinking, since all academic learning has a written text. And, of course, reading comprehension is one expression of general intelligence—a fact that frustrates teachers of street-bright, illiterate students: if Sheila is so bright on the playground, why isn't she doing well in school?

Active Learning: Teach students to generate questions from reading material.

Example: Janet Marcus has found that her sixth graders generally do not do assigned readings at home; however, most of her students are diligent about handing in written homework assignments on time. By asking students to generate questions from their reading assignments, she has made their reading at home more active—and more likely to occur.

When she assigns a new chapter, Ms. Marcus asks students to "translate" headings and subheadings into questions. To reduce the mechanical aspect of the task, she asks students to combine two or more headings into one question, or to make sure that many of their questions ask "Why?" and "How?"—which require more complex explanations than a definitional question asking "What?"

Discussion: Asking students to turn textbook headings and subheadings into questions may seem like a mechanical exercise: there will be many

"What is . . . ?" questions in the beginning. However, if you combine this exercise with some of the others suggested in this monograph, you will find students starting to ask better questions. When they think in terms of the kinds of questions being raised, their learning will be more goal-oriented.

We have just said that reading with comprehension involves looking for answers to your own questions. Therefore, the way to help students understand—and correctly interpret—what they are reading is to follow the behavior of good readers: students should generate their own questions and read to answer them. Here is a technique you may wish to introduce to your students:

1. *Survey the chapter.* Read the chapter summary, main headings and subheadings, and captions under some of the illustrations.
2. *Formulate questions.* Take a small section of the chapter and turn the headings and subheadings into questions. When writing the questions, relate headings and subheadings to each other, as well as to the chapter title. (For example, in a chapter titled "Westward Expansion," a heading might be "The Gold Rush." A good question would be, "How did the Gold Rush affect westward expansion?" not, "What was the Gold Rush?")
3. *Read to answer the questions.* When your students reach this step, ask them to look in the chapter for the answers to their questions. When they find the answers, ask them to write down keywords and phrases to help them remember the answers if asked to report them to others.

If a textbook heading or subheading covers several paragraphs, the prereading question may be too general. In this case, ask your students to—

1. Read only the first sentence of each paragraph. Find two or three keywords or phrases in each of these sentences.
2. Write a question that includes keywords from each first sentence. This question will summarize the author's argument, and help students—especially slow readers—read with comprehension. (Note: While this skill is especially useful to slow readers, it may require some individualized work—modeling the skill, talking aloud each sentence, keywords, and summary questions—before these students will be able to use it independently. You may want to involve your school's special education or remedial

reading consulting teacher in this activity, helping you individualize the skill for students whose reading is significantly below grade level.)

3. Read the whole passage. Does it answer the questions asked?

Discussion: It is true that first sentences are not always topic sentences. However, if students take important words from the first sentences of several paragraphs, they will form a general picture—create a hypothesis—about what the passage is saying. And since students are reading actively, looking for confirmation or denial of their hypothesis, even a "wrong" question is useful. For example, a student thinks that a given passage will talk about the general causes of the French Revolution and writes a question to be answered with such information. Actually the passage discusses the role of the aristocracy as a cause of the revolution. The student can revise his/her original question after reading the material to find the right answer. Nothing is lost—the student was actively pursuing a goal in reading for information, rather than passively turning pages until the chapter was "finished." Whether or not the student initially asked the "right" question of the material to be read, he or she used the approach of the scientist—making guesses, following them, making corrections when necessary. This is the essence of both critical and creative thinking. The student should not simply follow a straight path, looking for the "right" answers to the "right" (traditionally, the textbook's) questions. If the passage answers a slightly different question, the student should revise the original question. The point is to use the scientific method—make guesses, then follow them, sometimes into blind alleys, and then make corrections. Playing with, testing, revising ideas—these activities are central to active, critical thinking.

Passive Learning: Don't give students "reading comprehension" exercises—reading passages followed by questions—in an effort to improve reading comprehension.

Example: Myra is a sixth grader reading at fourth grade level. In the past year, working with the remedial reading teacher, her reading speed has improved somewhat, but her reading comprehension remains poor. It is clear that there is nothing wrong with Myra's intelligence: she is bright and lively, and scores well on oral comprehension tests.

Ms. Algard, the remedial reading teacher, has a number of reading comprehension exercise programs in her reading lab. All of them rely on the standard comprehension exercise: a passage followed by questions about the main idea, facts, and author's intent. Ms. Algard notices that students like Myra often improve their performance on these exercises, but they remain poor readers when they return to normal classroom assignments.

Discussion: If spoken or written discourse is a set of answers to implied questions, comprehension is the act of seeing the *connections* between consecutive questions/answers. In daily life a person is judged to be intelligent if he/she can carry on a conversation that has a common thread, even though it may veer off in different directions. For example, when Ted misses school on the day of an important test, he invents a story with many twists and turns to explain his absence. The connecting thread of the story—why he missed school and should not be blamed for it—suggests the workings of a creative, intelligent mind. Ted's intelligence is shown in other ways: he easily comprehends a complicated set of instructions from his football coach, and he readily follows the story line of a complex science fiction movie. However, Ted reads painfully slowly. He reads aloud with no expression and stumbles over words. His only goal seems to be getting to the end of a sentence. Whether reading silently or orally, by the time he reaches the end of a paragraph, he no longer knows what he has been reading about; he cannot see the relationship between successive paragraphs since he does not know what he has just read. Ted cannot use his out-of-school thinking skills when reading because the mechanics slow him down—he does not see the questions the paragraphs implicitly raise, or the connections between them.

Traditionally, Ted would be given exercises in "reading comprehension"—paragraphs followed by questions, similar in form to reading passages on the Scholastic Aptitude Tests. He may learn to skim for answers to the questions provided, and improve his performance on these exercises—particularly when questions deal with facts, as opposed to interpretations. However, when assigned a chapter in his history text, Ted encounters the same old problem: his attention wanders, his reading is slow and halting, he cannot recall the flow of ideas as he reads them.

What's wrong? Simply that "reading comprehension" exercises do not capture the activity critical to good readers: as they read they conduct an ongoing internal dialogue, they generate questions about what the material might contain, and they read for confirmation or denial of their hypotheses. Students who can read to answer their own questions can also read to answer the questions of others—those of a test maker or textbook writer. But it does not follow that the way to improve reading comprehension for students like Ted is to give them endless reading passage/question exercises.

3. *Finding models of good questions*

Active Learning: Ask students to hand in mock exam questions—some of which you will actually use in classroom quizzes and exams.

Example: Margaret Hood's tenth grade biology class has been studying muscle contraction. Students have conducted a lab experiment on frogs' legs, and have been assigned a textbook chapter on the operation of muscles. As part of the reading assignment, Ms. Hood asked students to turn in questions that were answered by information in the chapter. She promised to include a number of them in the quiz on muscles. Here are some questions students submitted:

Where does the energy come from that causes the muscle to expand and contract?

How does energy get to the muscle?

How are waste products taken away from muscles?

Discussion: Asking students to make up questions that you may use in actual tests has several advantages: (1) it enables you to help students discriminate between relevant and irrelevant questions (see #4, pp. 27–29) and to ask questions that increasingly approximate those of a professional; (2) it helps students take their question generating more seriously, so that they ask increasingly more complex questions that approximate yours; (3) it provides students with a specific, concrete reward for generating "good" questions.

Passive Learning: Don't rely heavily on textbook questions and workbook exercises.

Example: Harvey Borden teaches world culture to ninth graders. At first, the textbook chosen by his school looked ideal: chapters begin with a set of learning objectives, questions appear throughout and at the end of each chapter, important points are printed in italics or boldface type, paragraphs are short, and there are many illustrations. Students like the book and they score well on objective exam questions. However, they seem to forget material as soon as they have learned it, they have difficulty answering short-answer or essay questions not explicitly raised in the text, and they are unable to see relationships between material learned from different chapters. Mr. Borden suspects that his students are simply memorizing the answers to the questions printed in the book.

Discussion: In recent years, many textbook authors have made efforts to provide readers with a clear sense of their instructional objectives. For example, in a short chapter introduction they may indicate which questions the chapter will answer, and they may break up the chapter into sections, briefly summarizing each section with a list of key points and questions. There is nothing wrong with clear instructional objectives in themselves. However, too many aids of this kind can increase students' passivity: everything is set out for them; they read the chapter in the same lockstep, mechanical way they would use to follow a cookbook recipe.

If you want to help your students *think* while reading, use the author's aids as *models*. That is, read the author's objectives aloud, then page through the chapter with students; ask them to work in pairs, identifying which sections of the chapter provide the information for each of the author's objectives. Next, ask students to cover the objectives for the following chapter—one they have not read—and again, working in pairs, ask them to page through the chapter, this time coming up with their own list of objectives that they think the chapter will cover. Later, have them match their objectives with those of the author.

4. *Helping students improve question quality*

Active Learning: Make up handouts showing the differences between "good" and "poor" student-generated exam-type questions.

Example: Joe Stone teaches science in a junior high school. He wants to teach his students more than the facts of his discipline: he wants them to think of science as a way of testing out new ideas. In addition, he wants them to be able to write about their ideas and therefore integrates writing practice into most of his assignments and classroom work. He has noticed that his most creative students, who generate some of the most interesting hypotheses about the operation of a process under study, are not necessarily his best writers.

Mr. Stone frequently uses feedback sheets composed of student products. If a student hands in an assignment on which the creative work is particularly good, but the writing is poor, Mr. Stone gives suggestions for rewriting the assignment. When it is revised, he makes ditto master copies of the student's completed work and uses this as a basis for classroom discussion, pointing out those elements that he thinks are most important for student learning.

Students feel encouraged by Mr. Stone's use of their work as models. Interested in having their work shared by others, and hoping to avoid the step of revising their assignments, they exercise more thought and attention to detail in their written homework.

Discussion: When learning a new skill, everyone needs a model and a foil—examples of what the skill should and should *not* look like. Unfortunately, throughout formal education illustrations of models and foils are usually provided in ways that students find punishing or difficult to learn from. For example, teachers may mark all the errors on students' papers in an effort to provide feedback and to show them what their writing should *not* look like. And the "ideal" paper used as a model may be one written by the teacher, the class's best student, or by a textbook writer. Instead, students need *transitional* examples—foils with only one or two errors that are clear enough for students to identify and subsequently look for in their own work, and models drawn from average/good student samples that clearly exemplify properties students can add to their own work.

Passive Learning: Don't ask students to use the 5W question forms.

Example: George Peabody wants the students in his eleventh grade psychology class to understand more of what they are reading. He feels that they spend too much time memorizing information from the textbook just before a quiz. To improve this situation, he started asking students to generate questions from the text. Whenever a chapter is assigned, students are required to hand in questions that the text "answers." Mr. Peabody has specified that they use the Who? What? Why? When? Where? format for generating their questions. He is disappointed with the results: the students still seem to be learning the material by rote, in a mechanical, unquestioning manner.

Discussion: Not all question forms have the same weight. For example, the response to a "when" question can be one word; a "why" question requires a more complex response. It is most important to remember that you are *not* proceeding through a series of workbook exercises: the rationale for students' generating questions is to help them think more actively, more analytically, about the course material. For this reason, avoid creating a lockstep formula for their questions. Remember that your students are good at asking questions outside school—they are continually engaged in internal dialogues as they talk with the corner grocer, negotiate their way across crowded streets, and so on. You will be surprised at how quickly they will learn to ask good questions of the fields they are studying—the kinds of questions you think are important—if they translate the material at hand into the questions it answers. Here are some guidelines for students:

1. "What" questions are good for definitions (for example, What is an electron?). Use them only to define a new term.
2. After defining basic terms, the best question forms to use are "how" and "why." You will find that their answers call for information that will help your students see relationships between new facts they are learning.

5. *Using alternative class formats to encourage question generating*
Active Learning: Use small group projects to promote student question building.

Example: Because all of Ann Abrams's seventh graders read well below grade level, she has decided to use questioning techniques. In this way she can help her students see that, even with their limited reading skills, they can read for information in a research project.

In setting up the small groups, she follows these principles:

1. Each group will contain one member who can act as a resource person for the others in the group (that is, a student reading at or above fourth grade level).

2. When students ask the teacher questions that can be answered by the group, she will refer them to the group. The major point here is consistency: if Ms. Abrams tells students that they have all the information they need, she knows that she should not continue to answer questions.
3. There is no "best way" of making up groups: some students will work better if assigned to a group, others when they choose their own. However, once group assignments are made, they will remain the same throughout the year (barring strong conflicts that may arise within a group). Ms. Abrams realizes that the process of students' continually choosing and shifting groups can become a source of behavior problems.

For her unit on Africa, Ms. Abrams asked students to brainstorm, listing statements and questions about Africa. None of the statements needed to be true (for example, one statement was "Africa is a country."), but all had to be verifiable. She elicited these statements and questions from students during a recitation session, wrote them on the board, then built the unit as follows:

1. The class was split into small groups or research teams. Each team was to look for answers to questions class members had asked or to verify statements they had made. For four weeks, the teams spent the class period in the school library.
2. Each team researched a section of the statements to determine their truth or falsity. If false, students were to find the word that would make the statement true (for example, "Africa is a continent.").
3. Ms. Abrams arranged the students' questions into educational, geographic, agricultural, and linguistic categories (for example, What kind of crops do they grow? What do people hunt with?). Each team chose a category to research for a short report.
4. At the end of the month, Ms. Abrams gave an open-book test consisting of students' questions and statements. To answer the questions, students were encouraged to use each other's reports as resources.

Discussion: Questioning techniques can afford students independence as learners, so that they look for answers to their own questions and they begin to understand the information-source function of reading in personal terms. Using small group teams will help all students—even those with very poor skills—become actively involved in a research project.

A similar format might be used for more advanced classes. For example, students in a high school biology class might do team research, looking for answers to their own questions on issues such as the effects of acid rain.

Passive Learning: Don't use a recitation format for eliciting questions from students until they have had practice and success in generating questions through individual seatwork, small group work, and homework assignments.

Example: Ms. Lodge has just finished demonstrating to her fourth grade class how water vaporizes into steam. During the demonstration, she stood in front of the class lecturing on the process of vaporization while water in a curette visibly lowered and steam was given off. She now turns to her students and asks if they have any questions about the process they have seen and heard about. Jimmy asks, "Where did the water go to?" Ms. Lodge answers by repeating some key points she has just mentioned. Annoyed, feeling that perhaps a number of students have not paid attention to the demonstration, Ms. Lodge calls on students at random, asking questions that test their understanding of the concept "vaporization." Students answer haltingly, and Ms. Lodge feels as if she is pulling teeth.

Discussion: In most teaching situations, the recitation format results in student *passivity*—the opposite of the active learning environment that promotes critical thinking.* If the teacher calls on students randomly, some of the passive atmosphere is reduced. But it is replaced only in small part by the students' actively following, anticipating, and inter-

---

*In some cases recitation classes can promote active student involvement. For example, when students have had practice and have begun to achieve mastery in some of the skills suggested in this monograph, a decision-making or debate-oriented recitation class can result in lively participation (see pp. 39–41). However, it is important to lay the foundations for recitation classes so that more students than your "best" ones become involved.

nally answering the teacher's prompts. The major part of most students' internal dialogue in a recitation class involves emotional issues (for example, "Is the teacher going to call on me? How will I feel if I say the wrong thing and look foolish to the other kids?"). In addition, students who have never done well in school may simply turn off during recitation sessions; they learn to say "I don't know," and realize that others expect them to be "out of it."

Throughout this section, we have indicated that active learning occurs when students seek answers to field-relevant questions. Trying to promote this activity artificially—by randomly calling on students to respond before they have had time to "play" with the new concepts, to generate questions from them and make variations on them—often results in an uncomfortable contest of will between teacher and students.

IMAGINATIVE WRITING

As we have shown, student question writing is an important component of critical thinking. Writing their own questions helps students see the relationships among facts of a given field, helps them understand the field in terms of the questions it addresses. Above all, it promotes more *active learning*.

Imaginative writing is another kind of exercise that will help students think more actively. Its objective is to "loosen up" students, to help them talk to themselves on paper. Here are some imaginative writing exercises you may want to use in class:

Biology: Ask students to imagine a day in the life of an animal you are studying (an earthworm, a rabbit, an elephant). Working in pairs, ask students to raise questions about the animal: what it eats, sees, feels, how large it is in relation to specific parts of its environment. Facts need *not* be scientifically correct; later on students can use their books and library references to confirm their guesses.

English: Ask students to write about the first hour of waking up on a typical day last summer. What were the first things they heard and felt before opening their eyes (a barking dog, a sweaty bedsheet)? What was the first thing they saw? What did they feel when their feet touched the floor? Ask them to make sure that each sentence contains a *physical* description, not an emotional one (that is, the color "green," not a word like "beautiful"). How did the air feel? the floor? What were two or three things in the room they first noticed? After students have been writing for 15 minutes, ask them to exchange papers and work in pairs, circling the words that describe specific sensations in each other's work, prompting each other about what was left out but might be included.*

Social Studies: Your class has been studying ancient Rome. Ask students to work in pairs to answer the following questions: You are a citizen of the Roman republic. How do you feel about Caesar making himself emperor? How would you feel if this happened in America today?

Discussion: The imaginative (or creative) writing exercises described here are not "free writing": students are asked to write *something* in response to a general problem or question. We call this an imaginative writing exercise because we are not concerned here with factual truths or the structure of students' arguments.

What is the purpose of such an exercise? Each of our examples illustrates a problem faced by professionals in these fields. What questions should one examine when doing field research with animals? How should one write vivid descriptions? By not stating the problems formally, with "right" and "wrong" answers, we give students the chance to explore something about the field that the professional does: make guesses, test hypotheses, see how something will "work" without an immediate judgmental consequence. In a sense, we are teaching students to use a method of scientific inquiry. We are not summarizing, stating the 10 steps of a process found by the researcher after long months or years of experimentation. We are giving students a chance to explore wrong directions, to see where guesses might lead.

---

*See "Working in Pairs," pp. 37–38.

Aspects of Imaginative Writing:
Generating Questions and Keywords

Exercises that promote creative thought require some kind of structure: that is, there must be some point of departure, some way for the student to get started on the task. Here is a method that you might introduce during imaginative writing exercises, one that will also form the basis for students' writing formal essays and research papers. Give students a topic about which they already have opinions, can make guesses, or can use certain tools or analytic skills you have already introduced into the course. Examples for high school students might be, "Should the legal drinking age be raised to 21?" or "Should restrictions be placed on genetic research?" If students know little about the topic, but it is one that easily lends itself to a discussion of two sides of a controversy (like the question of genetic research), you may wish to give students some background by assigning a short magazine article on the issue. (The article should be short because you are trying to help students play with their own ideas, not facts. In other words, this exercise stresses the creative, rather than the translation, aspect of critical thinking.)

FEEDBACK: AN ESSENTIAL ASPECT OF ACTIVE LEARNING

Your goal as a teacher is to engage students actively in academic work so that they become involved in what they are learning, motivated by the excitement inherent in each field they study, avidly seeking answers to their own questions. The exercises we are suggesting in this monograph will help your students become active learners. However, one essential component is missing in all these exercises by themselves—and in those presented in many activity books. That is the element of ongoing feedback.

Feedback on progress is essential to all learning. Outside school, it is readily presented by the environment: we look for cars when crossing a street, we watch carefully while pouring juice into a glass—there are immediate consequences for inattention. Our learning is shaped by the environment: we learn to notice and make adjustments for changes. If a first approximation to a task is successful, we will take a chance on doing the task more quickly, or try a more difficult aspect of it.

However, if we receive inadequate feedback—feedback that is remote in time from the performance of a task, or that seems otherwise unrelated to it—we will not be changed by the feedback and will most likely repeat the same mistakes.

The feedback students receive in school often comes too long after the task to provide useful information. In addition, it is often too complex to be useful. If Janet makes 10 kinds of grammatical errors on a short paper, and all are marked in red by her teacher, she will not know where to begin to improve her writing. The paper is most likely a candidate for the round file.

Immediate feedback serves another role besides shaping learning: it is a powerful source of reinforcement and will keep students working long after other inducements have failed.

How does this relate to teaching critical thinking? Like any new skill, learning to think in an academic setting is difficult at first. Students will be anxious about their success, especially given their experience in school thus far. They will think, "Am I asking the 'right' questions? How many questions should I ask?" Over time, as critical thinking exercises make it easier for them to master a wide range of content-area course work,* students will find the use of critical thinking skills rewarding in themselves. And they will find ways to give themselves feedback on their success in using these skills. However, while they are engaged in the process of acquiring the skills, they will need feedback to shape their learning and to reinforce their use of the skills.

For all these reasons, if you decide to incorporate thinking skills into your teaching, make them "count"; give students credit toward their course grades for using the skills. *A good feedback system is essential to students' acquisition of these skills.*

Feedback That Improves Students' Performance

The best feedback systems have the following components: they provide direction and reinforcement to students; they give students ongoing, specific knowledge of their performance; they quickly follow tasks completed by students; and they are simple enough to be reinforcing to *teacher* as well as students.

What are some useful ways of providing this feedback? Teachers who are most effective at incorporating thinking skills into the classroom devise point systems for students' use of the skills. These systems

---

*Unlike critical learning skills from systems that are abstract and unrelated to content–course material, these exercises will not take your students away from the material of your course, and they will help you achieve your content–course instructional objectives.

35

should *not* be complicated—both for reasons of consistency and to reduce the teacher's "homework" time. In this connection, suppose you are asking your students to perform some of the question-generating exercises suggested in this monograph. What kind of marking system are you currently using? If 30 percent of the students' final grade is classwork, and you plan to introduce thinking skills into every class (during lectures, students take notes and generate questions from them; during group work, students perform a task involving question generating and decision making), then 30 percent of the grade is now students' classroom thinking work. If you also plan to ask students to perform homework exercises that, in part, require their use of thinking skills, you will want to count that work as part of the final grade.

How can you grade students' use of a thinking skill? As we have said, the best grading policy is one that is simple and consistent. When you plan to introduce a skill, decide how many points it is worth. For example, suppose you plan to ask students to write questions based on lectures and on readings (these may be exercises done in class or as homework assignments). Students may receive one point for every "what" question and three points for every "how" or "why" question. More complex questions—those that ask for examination of more than one aspect of a situation/fact/event—may receive five points each. This may seem simplistic because it does not allow for shades of difference in the quality of questions. However, we have found that this kind of point system is effective; it keeps students working at the task, and helps them improve their performance, while allowing the teacher the minimum of at-home marking time. *Do not introduce a grading system that you find cumbersome or time-consuming.* It will give you negative feelings about the task itself, and make it less likely that you will follow through with either consistent grading or practice of the skills themselves.

Whatever feedback system you plan to implement, remember that it must be rewarding to your students. All feedback, whether formal (a point system) or informal (a teacher's comments), should have the effect of encouraging student performance. If you expect too much too quickly of students, if you praise some students and not others, this training will have a negative impact on the class. The following elements are crucial to a useful feedback system:

1. Sequence the critical thinking activities to fit the progress of your students. There is no formal curriculum, no time chart, for

your critical thinking exercises. Unlike the content area you teach simultaneously, no specific amount of material must be covered by the end of the term. Thus you can introduce critical thinking skills at a pace that ensures skill mastery for most students.

2. *When commenting on students' individual work, be positive.* For example, if a student has made an effort to generate questions, but is not following instructions, do not say, "That's wrong." Find something positive to say about the student's work. This is especially important in the early stages of introducing critical thinking skills into your class. Most important, *be aware of individual effort and progress.* If you are walking around the room, glancing at students' work, comment on the progress of individuals. For example, if Freddy has generated five questions, only one of which reflects the material, tell him, "Freddy, that's a good question you asked about the Puritans." Further, let him know *why* it is a good question: "I can see that this question asks about the section of the textbook chapter that I assigned."

Use students' good work as models for improving their poorer work. To continue our example, once you have shown Freddy what is good about the one on-target question he generated, help him use that question as a model for improving his other questions. (You might point to an off-target question, saying, "Can you rewrite this question so that it would be a good test question for this passage, just as you did with the other question here?")

WORKING IN PAIRS

As we have said, critical thinking involves an ongoing internal dialogue on the part of the learner in which new ideas are compared to existing knowledge, hypotheses are raised and tested, and there is a continual play between questions raised and answered. The engaged learner is actively searching for information. In contrast, the disengaged learner is passive when faced with an academic task.

The active learner is also a good self-educator, aware of what the work product should look like and checking for accuracy. In contrast, the passive learner is impulsive, skipping over important information and gathering facts chaotically.

One device for helping students think more actively and systematically is to have them work in pairs when performing a wide variety of seatwork tasks, including the kinds of thinking exercises described in this monograph. We are, however, talking about a *structured* way of working in pairs. The model we are suggesting, based on the work of Whimbey and Lochhead (43), calls for students to alternate roles as problem solver and listener.

Working in pairs will improve students' active learning skills if they adopt the following behaviors as listeners and problem solvers:

- The *problem solver* thinks aloud, explaining each step taken. Thus if Rachel is solving a physics problem, she thinks aloud, first reading the problem, then searching for parts of it (isolating the unknown and the knowns, talking, recalling information, drawing illustrations that may aid in finding a solution, constructing or recalling a relevant formula, testing out the formula on the material at hand).

- The *listener* takes an active role in this process. Working with Rachel, Ben listens for gaps in her thinking: Did she leave out a step or overlook some information? Did she produce an illustration to help her toward solving the problem? If so, are there any obvious errors or inconsistences in the illustration? If Ben sees any errors or gaps, he asks *questions*, prompting Rachel to edit her own work. Ben does *not* give Rachel the solution, if he sees it before she does. When Ben and Rachel complete work on the problem at hand, they exchange roles and work on another.

By exchanging roles as problem solver and listener, students practice the criterion behavior: they explicitly model the internal dialogue roles that they will begin to internalize over time. The process allows for searching apparently blind alleys, in much the same way that a scientist pursues different methods of finding solutions to an unsolved problem. Students are not following an ordered, step-by-step process from problem to solution. Rather, by thinking aloud and checking each other's thinking, they are learning to generate and test hypotheses about the field at hand. This process, and other methods we have advocated, will result in active thinking; it will enable students to begin to solve unfamiliar problems in new contexts. In addition, it will improve their performance on complex, in-class exams.

THE SCIENTIFIC MODEL: EXPLORING STUDENTS' PROBLEM-SOLVING METHODS

In our discussion of working in pairs, we suggested that students look for their own methods of solving problems, even if these do not result in problem solution. This does not mean that students should be encouraged to see each new problem as distinct from those encountered in the past. It means that they should be allowed to consciously pursue a method of problem solving, being aware of the steps they are choosing during the process. In other words, if Dan, working with an actively listening partner, verbally justifies each step he takes in solving a given problem ("There are too many parts to hold in my head. I'm going to draw a diagram to see if I can understand it better."), he is thinking about the method he has chosen. When he gets stuck, his partner, Kathy, who is looking at a similar problem worked out in the textbook, might say, "I think you left out this part of the problem. Maybe you ought to try to figure out something about 'work' first. Do you remember how it was written in class?"

It is true that students may not find the most efficient way to solve problems—and sometimes they may not be able to solve a problem at all. However, at this point a more effective strategy will have meaning to them: it will answer a question they have generated in the course of looking for a workable strategy. Strategies for solving familiar problems that have been outlined by the textbook or the teacher will not be memorized, but understood logically.

The difference between this method and standard, plug-in-the-numbers practices will become clear when you imagine the questions that students in each situation might ask the teacher. In the more passive mode, the student might say, "I don't know how to do this problem." In the more active, strategy-seeking mode, the student will say, "I can see how to do this problem up to here, but then I get stuck."

DECISION MAKING

Exercises in "decision making" are central to a number of thinking programs. Such exercises usually have two main components:

1. They are organized in discussion or debate format.
2. They are organized around topics designed to encourage specific

thinking skills (creative, divergent thinking; comparative analysis; weighing alternatives; ordering priorities).

Such exercises can be valuable if students are properly *prepared* for them and if they are appropriately *sequenced*.

Preparation

As we noted earlier, it is difficult to involve the majority of students in any class in a recitation or discussion format: these classes tend to be dominated by a few highly verbal students and leave others worrying self-consciously about how well they will answer if they are called on.

If the discussion format is to result in active student participation, students must have practice in the requisite class-discussion subskills. If students have *generated questions* from class materials, done *imaginative writing* exercises, and worked in *problem solver/listener pairs*, they will be much more actively engaged during class discussions or debates.

Sequencing

We suggest sequencing discussion classes from content-free to academic, as follows:

1. In your first discussion class, try a deBono-type of content-free exercise (see p. 14), such as asking your students to consider what would happen if all cars were painted yellow. Such a topic is value-free, nonthreatening—has no "right" or "wrong" answers—and will therefore encourage student participation.

2. In your next discussion class, consider a topic that is potentially real, researchable, and interesting to students. (Ideas for this might be taken from blockbuster movies: What would happen if a major earthquake hit Los Angeles? if a nuclear bomb were dropped on New York City? if aliens invaded the earth and took over the governments of the superpowers?) Ask students to prepare for this class by working together in small groups, generating questions and answers about the topic you have chosen.

3. Assign each group some research activity related to the major questions raised. Following this research, bring the class together in a debate of the central questions surrounding the issue.

4. Your students are now ready to apply critical analysis skills to their decision-making discussion groups. You may want to assign different groups readings that—

40

- Require the comparison of two or more conflicting opinions on an important issue in a particular field. This will give students the opportunity to see that "authorities" do not always agree on a given topic.
- Contain subtle forms of propaganda.
- Challenge students' existing ideas by providing unexpected information.

Issues forming the basis of discussions might be interdisciplinary, involving a project done for more than one course. For example, students in both earth sciences and social studies classes might study the effects of toxic waste on a community.

GENERATING EXAMPLES

Objective: When students encounter new terms in lectures or readings, they will skim for an example, generate their own example, and formulate a definition for the term.

Example: Adele Scott is teaching a course in law to ninth graders. During a lecture on types of crime, she asks students to list in their notebooks the terms and definitions she is mentioning. Some terms, such as "arson," are easily definable. Others, such as "aggravated assault," must be more fully explained. When defining such terms, Ms. Scott cites an example, which her students dutifully copy in their notebooks. However, the class quickly achieves a more active dimension: when her brief lecture is over, Ms. Scott asks her students, working in pairs, to write their *own* examples of each term that she has defined by example. The students then share their examples with each other in a recitation format. In their notebooks they make a glossary of these terms, each defined by example.

Ms. Scott asks students to proceed through a similar exercise when they encounter complex new concepts in their textbooks.

Discussion: The assumption that concepts can—and should—be taught at the abstract level as students approach the upper elementary and high school years ignores the idea of learning as an ongoing internal dialogue. In other words, learners who apparently deal easily and well with purely abstract concepts do so because they have *experience* in testing out similar ideas on reality. For example, $E = mc^2$ did not suddenly spring from Einstein's mind: he had conducted thought experiments for years, imagining the concrete effects of relative variations on the speed of moving objects. And these objects were not themselves abstract: he thought in terms of trains and whistles—objects he had long experience with and whose behavior in varying circumstances he could readily predict.

Not only is teaching done on an abstract level, *what* is taught—the concepts themselves—are often summarized rules that researchers have discovered under trial-and-error experimentation. That is, students are often not taught to use the scientific process of exploration and discovery; rather, they are asked to memorize facts, rules, and concepts that are apparently set in stone.

This emphasis on abstract concepts and summarized rules has very little relation to active learning and critical thinking—the kind of learning that most students do *outside* the classroom. When students learn in nonacademic settings, they do so through an active process: they are continually forming hypotheses about what they see and hear. As we noted earlier, learners are shaped by feedback in the environment, which occurs from infancy onward. Through trial-and-error experimentation, babies learn that they are less likely to fall if they shift their weight while walking. Similarly, engineers may learn that a particular experiment will yield results given an adjustment in the force or weight of an object. Of course, engineers have a history of hypothesis-testing, and add to their calculations the accumulated knowledge—verified hypotheses—of others in the field. But the process in both cases—the consequences of the specific actions taken—is much the same, and is critical to shaping the learner's competence.

This lesson is very clear to teachers of the early elementary grades. They do not present concepts in abstract forms; they see concrete illustration as central to learning. Somehow this lesson is often forgotten as students move into the upper grades. It is assumed that older students can grasp abstract concepts that are not expressed in concrete form, that may in fact be outside their experience. There is some reason to think this may be so: after all, can't "smart" people work out complex problems in their heads? Of course they can—but only because they have learned how to learn—because they are constantly generating questions about the world, comparing new information with what they have learned, revising assumptions on the basis of new data.

CONCLUSION

In this monograph we have attempted to provide teachers with a practical guide to introducing critical thinking skills into the classroom. We have talked about thinking as a set of skills that, like other skills, can be improved through practice. We have attempted to demystify the higher-level learning process, asking teachers to reflect on the steps they engage in when working through a complex problem: What questions does the problem pose? What clues are there toward its solution? Complex problems may be academic (reading through a difficult journal article) or personal/social (telling a child about a prospective divorce). In all cases, they require a systematic, ongoing internal dialogue if they are to be resolved successfully. It is this process that we have defined as critical thinking; the exercises in this monograph are designed to stimulate and encourage this process in the student.

We hope that you will use these exercises in an open-ended, experimental way. Try them out as suggested. Do they work? Do they need special modifications to fit your students' needs? Take progress data so that you know what is working—and what needs alteration. Finally, we suggest that you share your experiments with your colleagues. Some years ago, one of the authors acted as a consultant at an elementary school. Helping teachers individualize instruction, using available classroom materials, the consultant became a catalyst for teachers at the school to talk with each other about their efforts in this direction. Only then did one of the target teachers learn that her neighbor in the next classroom had been experimenting with individualization for several years! Don't let this happen to you—find out what other people in your school are doing about thinking, and share your ideas with them. Don't wait until an outsider comes in before you learn from and with each other.

BIBLIOGRAPHY

1. Andre, M. E. D. A., and Anderson, T. "The Development and Evaluation of a Self-Questioning Study Technique." *Reading Research Quarterly* 14, no. 4 (1978–79): 605–23.
2. Andre, T., and Sola, J. "Imagery, Verbatim and Paraphrased Questions, and Retention of Meaningful Sentences." *Journal of Educational Psychology* 68 (1976): 661–69.
3. Bergmann, S., and Rudman, G. J. *Decision-Making Skills for Middle School Students.* Washington, D.C.: National Education Association, 1985.
4. Bloom, B. S., and Broder, L. *Problem-Solving Processes of College Students.* Chicago: University of Chicago Press, 1950.
5. Bretherton, I., and others. "Individual Differences at 20 Months: Analytic and Holistic Strategies in Language Acquisition." *Journal of Child Language* 10, no. 2 (June 1983): 293–320.
6. Bruner, J. *The Process of Education.* Cambridge, Mass: Harvard University Press, 1960.
7. Buzan, T. *Use Both Sides of Your Brain.* New York: E. P. Dutton, 1976.
8. Cleland, C. J. "The Reading Clinic: Designing a Successful Experience for Students." *Reading World* 22, no. 2 (December 1983): 160–62.
9. Clement, J. "Mapping a Student's Causal Conceptions from a Problem-Solving Protocol." In *Cognitive Process Instruction*, edited by J. Lochhead and J. Clement, pp. 133–46. Philadelphia: Franklin Institute Press, 1979.
10. Cooper, P., and Stewart, L. *Language Skills in the Classroom.* Washington, D.C.: National Education Association, 1982.
11. deBono, E. *Teaching Thinking.* London: Maurice Temple Smith, 1976.
12. deLisi, R. "Developmental and Individual Differences in Children's Representation of the Horizontal Coordinate." *Merrill-Palmer Quarterly* 29, no. 2 (April 1983): 179–96.
13. Felker, D. B., and Dapra, R. A. "Effects of Question Type and Question Placement on Problem-Solving Ability in Prose Material." *Journal of Educational Psychology* 67 (1975): 380–84.
14. Feuerstein, R. *Instrumental Enrichment.* Baltimore: University Park Press, 1979.
15. _____, and Hoffman, M. *Teacher's Guide to the Feuerstein Instrumental Enrichment Program.* Baltimore: University Park Press, 1980.
16. _____, and others. "Instrumental Enrichment; An Intervention Program for Structural Cognitive Modifiability in Low Functioning Adolescents." *Proceedings of the NIE-LRDC Conference on Thinking and Learning Skills*, Washington, D.C., October 1980.

17. Frase, L. T. "Questions as Aids to Reading: Some Research on Theory." *American Educational Research Journal* 5 (1968): 319–32.
18. _____, and Schwartz, B. J. "Effect of Question Production and Answering on Prose Recall." *Journal of Educational Psychology* 67 (1975): 628–35.
19. Gray, R. L. "Toward Observing That Which Is Not Directly Observable." In *Cognitive Process Instruction*, edited by J. Lochhead and J. Clement, pp. 217–27. Philadelphia: Franklin Institute Press, 1979.
20. Greeno, J. G. "A Study of Problem Solving." In *Advances in Instructional Psychology*, edited by R. Glaser, pp. 13–73. Hillsdale, N.J.: L. Erlbaum Associates, 1978.
21. _____, and others. "Conceptual Competencies and Children's Counting." *Cognitive Psychology* 16, no. 1 (January 1984): 94–143.
22. Heiman, M. "Learning to Learn." In *Resource Book on Thinking Skills*, edited by A. Costa. Washington, D.C.: Association for Supervision and Curriculum Development, in press.
23. _____, and Slomianko, J. *Learning to Learn: Some Questions and Answers.* Cambridge, Mass.: Learning Skills Consultants, 1984.
24. Howes, M., and Morgan, V. "Intentionality and Field Dependence in Children's Moral Judgments." *British Journal of Educational Psychology* 53, no. 2 (June 1983): 170–74.
25. Hunter, J., and others. "Project SOAR: Teaching Cognitive Skills in a Pre-College Program." *Journal of Learning Skills* 1 (1982): 24–26.
26. Kelly, J. *Student-Centered Teaching for Increased Participation.* Washington, D.C.: National Education Association, 1985.
27. Larkin, J. H. "Information Processing Models and Science Instruction." In *Cognitive Process Instruction*, edited by J. Lochhead and J. Clement, pp. 109–18. Philadelphia: Franklin Institute Press, 1979.
28. Lin, H. "Approaches to Clinical Research in Cognitive Process Instruction." In *Cognitive Process Instruction*, edited by J. Lochhead and J. Clement, pp. 11–32. Philadelphia: Franklin Institute Press, 1979.
29. Lochhead, J., and Clement, J., eds. *Cognitive Process Instruction: Research on Teaching Thinking Skills.* Philadelphia: Franklin Institute Press, 1979.
30. Peck, J. E. *Critical Thinking and Education.* New York: St. Martin's Press, 1981.
31. Rothkopf, E. Z. "Variable Adjunct Question Schedules, Interpersonal Interaction, and Incidental Learning from Written Material." *Journal of Educational Psychology* 63 (1972): 87–92.
32. _____, and Bloom, R. D. "Effects of Interpersonal Interaction on the Instructional Value of Adjunct Questions in Learning from Written Material." *Journal of Educational Psychology* 61 (1970): 417–22.

33. Ryan, E. B., and others. "Effects of Semantic Integration Training on the Recall of Pictograph Sentences by Children in Kindergarten and First Grade." *Journal of Educational Psychology* 76, no. 3 (June 1984): 387–98.
34. Smith, A. E. "The Effectiveness of Training Students to Generate Their Own Questions Prior to Reading. *National Reading Council* 22 (1973): 71–77.
35. Tchudi, S. N., and Huerta, M. C. *Teaching Writing in the Content Areas: Middle School/Junior High.* Washington, D.C.: National Education Association, 1983.
36. _____, and Tchudi, S. J. *Teaching Writing in the Content Areas: Elementary School.* Washington, D.C.: National Education Association, 1983.
37. _____, and Yates, J. *Teaching Writing in the Content Areas: Senior High School.* Washington, D.C.: National Education Association, 1983.
38. Torrance, E. P. *Creativity in the Classroom.* Washington, D.C.: National Education Association, 1977.
39. Wales, C. E., and Stageer, R. A. *The Guided Design Approach.* Englewood Cliffs, N.J.: Educational Technology Publications, 1978.
40. Whimbey, A. *Intelligence Can Be Taught.* New York: E. P. Dutton, 1975.
41. _____. "Conversation with Arthur Whimbey." *Journal of Learning Skills* 1, no. 2 (Winter 1982): 14–22.
42. _____. "Teaching Analytical Reasoning in Mathematics." In *Cognitive Process Instruction*, edited by J. Lochhead and J. Clement, pp. 309–14. Philadelphia: Franklin Institute Press, 1979.
43. _____, and Lochhead, J. *Problem Solving and Comprehension.* Philadelphia: Franklin Institute Press, 1981.
44. Wilen, W. W. *Questioning Skills, for Teachers.* Washington, D.C.: National Education Association, 1982.

THINKING SKILLS PROGRAMS

The following programs are commercially available to schools interested in improving students' thinking skills. Many of the programs will make their instructional materials available only to schools where teachers have participated in a one- to two-day training workshop.

Black, H., and Black, S., eds. *Thinking Works.* (A clearinghouse for thinking skills materials for reading comprehension, gifted education, mathematics instruction, computer programming and software, and logic for children.) Published by and available from Thinking Works, P.O. Box 468, St. Augustine, FL 32085-0468.

Evans, W. K., and Applegate, T. P. *Making Rational Decisions.* (A program for helping high school students in the decision-making process. Students learn to define problems, prioritize concerns, assess sources; exercises relate to the social sciences.) Available from Prodec, Inc., Salt Lake City, Utah.

Feuerstein, R. *Instrumental Enrichment.* (A system of teaching abstract reasoning skills through the mediated learning process; intended for junior and senior high school students who are retarded performers.) Available from Curriculum Development Associates, Inc., Suite 414, 1211 Connecticut Ave., NW, Washington, DC 20036.

Fraenkel, J. R. *Helping Students Think and Value.* (Text offering a number of teaching strategies to help students improve concept development.) Available from Prentice-Hall, Englewood Cliffs, NJ.

Greenes, C. E., and others. *Problem-Mathics* and *Successful Problem Solving Techniques.* (Two texts offering a variety of math problems and detailed explanations of their solutions; emphasize problem-solving process; intended for junior and senior high school students.) Available from Creative Publications, Palo Alto, CA 94303.

Harnadek, A. *Critical Thinking, Books 1 & 2.* (Texts designed to provide practical learning exercises on a variety of topics related to thoughful decision making; intended for junior and senior high school students.) Available from Midwest Publications, P.O. Box 448, Pacific Grove, CA 93950.

Heiman, M., and Slomianko, J. *Learning to Learn.* (An instructional package for improving reasoning skills across the curriculum; students learn to apply new strategies directly to their academic work; intended for junior and senior high school students.) Available from Learning Skills Consultants, Box 493, Cambridge, MA 02138.

Modest, D. (project director). *SAGE.* (A program designed to develop higher-level thinking skills and critical thinking skills in intellectually gifted elementary students in grades 1–5.) Available from Project SAGE, Framingham Public Schools, 454 Water St., Framingham, MA 01701.

Whimbey, A., and Lochhead, J. *Problem Solving and Comprehension.* (A course designed to improve students' analytical reasoning; strong impact on learning in sciences and mathematics; intended for grades 9–12 and college-level students.) Available from Franklin Institute Press, 20th and Race Sts., Box 2266, Philadelphia, PA 19103.

Wildman, T. *Measuring Human Reasoning: A Review of Tests.* (Analysis of tests currently available to measure students' reasoning. Groups tests in following major categories: general tests of critical thinking, specific tests for logic, structure of intellect, learning style, Piagetian developmental tasks.) Available from the Center for Reasoning Studies, Virginia Polytechnic Institute and State University, Blacksburg, VA 24061.

Young, D. B. (project co-director). F.A.S.T. (Foundational Approaches in Science Teaching). (Designed to teach concepts and methods of physical, biological, and earth sciences and their relations to environment; intended for grades 6–8.) Available from F.A.S.T., University of Hawaii, College of Education, CRDG, 1776 University Ave., Honolulu, HI 96822.